Freedom from Fear & Depression

100+ CBT-Based Tools and Exercises to Find Emotional Freedom

DR. ABHIJIT SHARMA

ISBN- 978-93-343-8675-2
Publishing Year 2025

Freedom from Fear & Depression

100+ CBT-Based Tools and Exercises to Find Emotional Freedom

DR. ABHIJIT SHARMA

About the Author & Acknowledgements

I was born and raised in the beautiful states of Assam and Meghalaya, India. My father was a banker, and my mother was the daughter of an NRI doctor. Unfortunately, my parents separated during my early childhood, and my mother never came to see me again. My father, busy with his career, would occasionally visit, I lived mostly in hostels or rented accommodations. During this time, my relatives showed little interest in taking responsibility for me, leaving me to face a lonely, unwanted existence. This led me to become a victim of anxiety and depression.

Throughout my life, I have searched tirelessly for happiness. I immersed myself in research, reading around 700 books on the subject. Eventually, I uncovered the secrets to happiness, and by applying them to my life, I was able to transform my life completely. The exercises shared in this book have been integral to my personal journey. Today, I am a rich and successful businessman, surrounded by friends, well-wishers, and the respect of my relatives, who now seek my advice.

I am deeply grateful to everyone who has come into my life, as each person has taught me invaluable lessons. I would like to express my heartfelt thanks to Dr. Deepak Kelkar and Dr. Manish Sethi Jain, whose participation in the transformative Magic workshop was pivotal to my growth. I am also indebted to my mentor, Mr. Pradeep Kumar, whose guidance inspired me to read regularly. A special thank you to my wonderful wife, Papari, who has taught me countless lessons, and to my two amazing children, Dhun and Jiu, for bringing so much joy into my life.

I am eternally grateful to my friends, relatives, in-laws for their unwavering love and support. Lastly, I thank God and the beauty of nature for helping me train my brain to embrace happiness in any circumstance.

Thank you, thank you, thank you.

Dr. Abhijit Sharma

Table of Contents

About the Author & Acknowledgements 4

Chapter 1 10

The Invisible Prison: Understanding Your Mind's Chains 10

Practical Exercises 18

Key Lessons from This Chapter 21

Chapter 2 22

Rewiring Your Brain for Courage 22

Practical Exercises 30

Key Lessons from This Chapter 32

Chapter 3 33

The Anchor Method: Finding Safety in the Storm 33

Practical Exercises for Chapter 3 40

Key Lessons from This Chapter 42

Chapter 4 43

Silence the Inner Critic, Unleash the Inner Coach 43

Practical Exercises for Chapter 4 51

Key Lessons from This Chapter 53

Chapter 5 54

Gratitude as a Weapon Against Darkness 54

Practical Exercises for Chapter 5 61

Key Lessons from This Chapter 62

Chapter 6 63

The Fear Ladder: Turning Panic into Power....................63

Practical Exercises for Chapter 6...................................70

Key Lessons from This Chapter 72

Chapter 7 73

Movement and the Mind: How Motion Heals Emotion73

Practical Exercises for Chapter 7...................................79

Key Lessons from This Chapter 80

Chapter 8 81

The Power of Connection: Relationships as Lifelines ...81

Practical Exercises for Chapter 8...................................87

Key Lessons from This Chapter 88

Chapter 9 89

The Warrior's Mindset: Resilience Over Perfection......89

Practical Exercises for Chapter 9...................................95

Key Lessons from This Chapter 96

Chapter 11 97

The Power of Self-Compassion: Being on Your Own Side 97

Practical Exercises for Chapter 11...............................103

Key Lessons from This Chapter 104

Chapter 12 105

Rewriting Your Inner Story: Changing the Script of Your Life 105

Practical Exercises for Chapter 12....111

Key Lessons from This Chapter 112

Chapter 13 113

Mindfulness in Motion: Finding Calm in the Present..113

Practical Exercises for Chapter 13....119

Key Lessons from This Chapter 120

Chapter 14 121

Building Your Safe Haven: Creating Environments That Heal....121

Practical Exercises for Chapter 14....127

Key Lessons from This Chapter 128

Chapter 15 129

The Courage to Let Go: Releasing What No Longer Serves You....129

Practical Exercises for Chapter 15....136

Key Lessons from This Chapter 137

Chapter 16 – The Power of Hope: Lighting the Path Forward....138

Practical Exercises for Chapter 16....144

Key Lessons from This Chapter 145

Chapter 17 146

Living With Purpose: Turning Pain Into Power 146

Practical Exercises for Chapter 17 153

Key Lessons from This Chapter 154

Chapter 18 – The Ripple Effect: How Your Healing Helps the World 155

Practical Exercises for Chapter 18 162

Key Lessons from This Chapter 163

Conclusion – A New Beginning 165

This is your new beginning. Live it fully 172

Chapter 1

The Invisible Prison: Understanding Your Mind's Chains

***"Fear is the prison. Hope is the key."* – Unknown**

****The Prison You Can't See****

We all know what a physical prison looks like—tall stone walls, iron bars, guards with keys jingling at their waists. But there is another kind of prison that cannot be seen with the eyes. It has no walls, no bars, no guards. And yet, millions of people live inside it every single day.

This is the **invisible prison** of fear and depression.

It doesn't lock your body.

It locks your mind.

When you are trapped inside, every day feels like walking through deep water with heavy clothes on.

Your body moves, but your spirit feels weighed down.

Fear stands in one corner, whispering:

"Something bad is going to happen..."

Depression answers from the other:

"Nothing good will ever happen..."

The walls of this prison are built from worry, hopelessness, and self-doubt. And the cruelest thing is—you start believing you will never be free.

But you can.

Anjali's Story: The Day the Walls Closed In

Anjali was a bright, cheerful woman in her early thirties. She loved her job as a schoolteacher, spent weekends with friends, and enjoyed long walks in the park.

One rainy evening, she was on her way home when she was caught in a minor car accident. Nobody was badly hurt, but the shock shook her deeply. That night, she kept thinking, *"What if I had died? What if something worse happens tomorrow?"*

At first, she thought the feeling would pass. But weeks later, she still felt nervous every time she left home. She stopped driving. Soon, she avoided even short walks to the store.

The fear had built its first wall.

Then came the second wall—depression.

Since she was home all day, she lost touch with friends. She felt lonely, unmotivated, and worthless. She would lie in bed thinking, *"What's the point? My life is over."*

In less than three months, the invisible prison had surrounded her completely.

But here's the good news—Anjali didn't stay there forever. With the right tools, guidance, and daily actions, she slowly broke down those walls. Her journey began with understanding **what** was happening inside her mind.

And that's where your journey begins too.

Meet the Two Guards: Fear and Depression

Think of fear and depression as two guards in this invisible prison.

Fear – The Overprotective Guard

Fear is not always bad. It is your body's alarm system, designed to protect you from danger. If you're crossing a busy road and a car speeds toward you, fear floods your body with adrenaline so you can jump out of the way.

The problem begins when fear becomes **overprotective**. Instead of keeping you safe, it keeps you trapped. It starts sounding the alarm when there's no real danger—only imagined "what if" situations.

***"Fear doesn't stop death. It stops life."* – Unknown**

Depression – The Silent Guard

Depression works differently. It doesn't shout. It whispers lies:

* "You're not good enough."

* "Nothing will ever change."

* "Why even try?"

It drains your energy, numbs your emotions, and convinces you that escape is impossible.

***"Depression is like a war. You either win or die trying."* – Anonymous**

The Fear-Depression Loop

Fear and depression are partners in crime.

1. Fear triggers anxiety, making you avoid situations.

2. Avoidance leads to isolation and inactivity.

3. Inactivity fuels depression.

4. Depression makes you even more fearful of trying again.

And so the loop continues—day after day, month after month—unless you **break it**.

Why Awareness is the First Key

You cannot break free from a prison you don't realize you're in.

The **first step** is awareness.

Awareness means you stop saying, *"I am fear"* or *"I am depression"* and start saying, *"I experience fear"* or *"I feel depression."*

This tiny shift creates a gap between **you** and the problem. It helps you see that you are **not** your fear or depression—you are the person who can walk out of the prison.

"You are not the voice in your head. You are the one who hears it." – Michael A. Singer

How the Prison Was Built: Common Triggers

Fear and depression rarely appear without cause. Some common triggers are:

1. **Past Trauma** – abuse, accidents, betrayal, or loss.

2. **Long-Term Stress** – financial struggles, toxic workplaces, chronic health issues.

3. **Sudden Change** – divorce, job loss, moving to a new place.

4. **Negative Self-Image** – years of self-criticism and comparison.

5. **Isolation** – lack of supportive relationships.

Understanding your triggers is like finding the first loose brick—it gives you a place to start breaking the wall.

Naming the Guards: Why It Works

One of the most effective ways to weaken fear and depression is to **name them**.

Why? Because what you name, you can tame.

When you say, *"I feel fear in my chest right now,"* you separate yourself from the feeling. It's no longer your entire identity—it's just something passing through you.

Mini Story:

A man in therapy called his depression "The Heavy Fog." Every morning, he would say, *"The Heavy Fog is here today."* Over time, he noticed that the fog came and went—it was never permanent. This gave him hope.

Your First Loose Brick

Every prison wall has a weakness. For many people, it's the moment they **choose** to stop fighting themselves and start understanding themselves.

Right now, you may feel hopeless. But remember: hopelessness is just another lie depression tells. You have already taken the first step—by reading these words and wanting something better.

***"Once you become aware of the prison, you've already started walking toward the door."* – Unknown**

Practical Exercises

****Exercise 1 – Fear & Mood Tracker****

For the next 7 days:

1. Write down moments when you feel fear or sadness.

2. Note the trigger (thought, person, place, or memory).

3. Rate its intensity from 1–10.

4. Write one thing you did—or could have done—to calm yourself.

****Exercise 2 – Name Your Enemy****

Choose a name for your fear and your depression.

Examples:

* Fear: "The Overprotective Guard" or "The Alarm Bell."

* Depression: "The Heavy Fog" or "The Silent Weight."

When they show up, greet them by name:

"Ah, the Heavy Fog is here again. But it won't stay forever."

Exercise 3 – The 5-Minute Awareness Practice

Once a day, sit quietly for 5 minutes and ask:

* "What am I feeling right now?"

* "Where do I feel it in my body?"

* "Can I watch it without judging it?"

Write down your answers.

Exercise 4 – Your First Loose Brick

Write one empowering sentence about your situation:

* "I am not my fear."

* "I am stronger than this prison."

* "I can take small steps toward freedom."

Repeat it every morning for 7 days.

Bedtime Reflection Prayer (Optional)

*"Dear God,

Help me see that fear and depression are not who I am.

Show me the first brick I can remove from this prison.

Give me courage to take the next step tomorrow.

Amen."*

Key Lessons from This Chapter

* Fear and depression create an invisible prison—but you are not the prison.

* Fear is an overprotective guard that keeps you from living.

* Depression is a silent guard that drains hope.

* The fear–depression loop keeps you stuck unless you interrupt it.

* Awareness and naming your feelings are the first steps toward freedom.

In the next chapter, we will discover **how to rewire your brain for courage** so that fear loses its grip, depression loosens its hold, and you begin to feel safe in your own mind again.

Chapter 2

Rewiring Your Brain for Courage

"Courage is not the absence of fear, but the triumph over it." – Nelson Mandela

Why Courage Feels Impossible When You're Afraid

When you're trapped in fear and depression, "be brave" can sound like a cruel joke.

You might think:

* "If I could be brave, I wouldn't feel like this in the first place."

* "Courage is for strong people, not for someone like me."

But here's the truth: **Courage is not a gift you are born with. It is a skill you can train, just like a muscle.**

And your brain—yes, even *your* brain—can be rewired to think and act more courageously, no matter how afraid or hopeless you feel right now.

This chapter will show you how.

Your Brain: The Hardware and the Software

Think of your brain like a smartphone.

* The **hardware** is your physical brain—neurons, synapses, and chemical messengers.

* The **software** is your thought patterns, beliefs, and habits.

Fear and depression are like a virus in your phone—they keep running in the background, draining your energy and slowing you down.

But here's the good news: **Neuroplasticity**—your brain's ability to change—means you can install new "software" and train your mind to think differently.

"The brain is like a muscle. When it is exercised, we feel good. Understanding is joy." – Carl Sagan

The Fear Alarm System

Your brain has an ancient alarm system—the **amygdala**—that's designed to detect danger and prepare you to fight, flee, or freeze.

It was incredibly useful when humans lived in caves and faced lions. But in modern life, the amygdala sometimes goes off even when there's no lion—just a stressful meeting, a social gathering, or a memory of a past failure.

When the amygdala is in overdrive, you live in constant fear.

When depression joins in, it convinces you there's no point in trying.

Rewiring your brain is about **teaching your alarm system to relax** and **training your thoughts to support you instead of sabotage you**.

Mini Story: The Soldier Who Couldn't Leave the Battle

Raj, a soldier, came home after years of serving in dangerous zones. Even though he was safe, his body didn't believe it. Loud noises made him jump. Crowds made him sweat. He couldn't sleep without nightmares.

His therapist explained:

"Your brain is like a guard dog that's been barking for years. It doesn't know the war is over. We have to retrain it to rest."

Through breathing exercises, gradual exposure, and changing his thought patterns, Raj slowly taught his brain to stop reacting to false alarms. His story proves that even the most "wired" brains can be rewired.

Step 1 – Calm the Alarm Before You Rewire

You can't think clearly when your fear alarm is blaring. Before we change thought patterns, we need to signal safety to the brain.

Here's how to do it:

1. The 3–3–3 Breath

* Inhale for 3 seconds.

* Hold for 3 seconds.

* Exhale for 3 seconds.

Repeat 3 times. This slows your heartbeat and tells your brain, *"We're safe."*

2. Grounding Through the Senses

Notice:

* 5 things you can see

* 4 things you can touch

* 3 things you can hear

* 2 things you can smell

* 1 thing you can taste

These techniques pull you out of fearful thoughts and into the present moment.

Step 2 – Challenge the Fear Story

Fear and depression often run on stories:

* “If I try, I’ll fail.”

* “People will laugh at me.”

* “I can’t handle it.”

Rewiring starts with questioning those stories. Ask yourself:

* “Is this always true?”

* “What evidence do I have against it?”

* “If my best friend said this, what would I tell them?”

You will notice that most fear stories are based on assumptions, not facts.

"Don’t believe everything you think."* – Unknown

Step 3 – Install the Courage Circuit

Your brain gets better at whatever it repeats. If you constantly repeat fearful avoidance, you strengthen the fear circuit. If you repeat small acts of courage, you strengthen the courage circuit.

Here's how to do it:

1. **Start Tiny** – Instead of "I'll conquer all my fears today," pick one small action. If you fear social situations, start by smiling at one stranger.

2. **Repeat Daily** – Consistency builds new neural pathways.

3. **Celebrate Wins** – Every small act of courage deserves recognition—write it down, tell someone, or reward yourself.

Step 4 – Visualize the Victory

Athletes use visualization to prepare for games. Your brain responds to imagined experiences almost like real ones.

The Courage Visualization

1. Close your eyes.

2. Picture yourself in a fearful situation.

3. Imagine yourself acting calmly and confidently.

4. Feel the relief and pride as if it already happened.

Practice for 2 minutes daily to train your brain to expect courage, not fear.

Step 5 – Pair Action With Emotion

The strongest rewiring happens when you combine **action** with **positive emotion**.

Example: If you fear public speaking, practice speaking in front of a supportive friend who cheers you on. The emotional reward will help your brain associate the action with safety.

Practical Exercises

Exercise 1 – The Courage Journal

For 14 days, write down:

* One thing that scared you.
* What you did (or didn't do) about it.
* How you felt afterward.

Over time, you'll see patterns and progress.

Exercise 2 – The 3–3–3 Breathing Habit

Set a reminder on your phone to practice the 3–3–3 breath three times a day, even if you're not afraid. You're teaching your brain calm as a default state.

Exercise 3 – Daily Courage Challenge

Write down 10 small fears (from smallest to biggest). Tackle one each day for the next 10 days. Start tiny—success builds momentum.

****Exercise 4 – Visualization Practice****

Every morning, spend 2 minutes visualizing yourself calmly handling something you usually avoid. Smile as you do it.

Key Lessons from This Chapter

* Courage is a skill, not a personality trait.

* Neuroplasticity means your brain can be retrained.

* Calm the alarm first, then rewire thought patterns.

* Small, repeated acts of courage create lasting change.

* Visualization and positive emotion speed up rewiring.

In the next chapter, we'll discover *The Anchor Method*—how to create a powerful "mental safety rope" you can hold on to whenever fear or depression tries to pull you under.

Chapter 3

The Anchor Method: Finding Safety in the Storm

"You can't stop the waves, but you can learn to surf."* – Jon Kabat-Zinn

When the Storm Hits

Fear and depression often feel like being caught in a violent storm at sea.

One moment, you're in calm waters.

The next, huge waves crash over you, the wind howls, and you can't even see the shore.

In that moment, your thoughts race:

* "I'm going under."

* "This is too much."

* "I can't survive this."

When panic or hopelessness takes over, you feel like a small boat with no anchor—tossed around by the storm, powerless to control where you end up.

But here's the truth:

The waves are not the problem. The lack of an anchor is.

Mini Story: The Fisherman Who Never Sank

In a small coastal village, there was an old fisherman named Ravi. He'd been through more storms than anyone else in the village. One day, a young fisherman asked him, *"How do you always come back safely, no matter how bad the storm gets?"*

Ravi smiled and said, *"When the waves get rough, I don't fight them. I drop my anchor. The sea can roar all it wants, but I stay grounded until the storm passes."*

That's what we're going to do for your mind.

What Is a Mental Anchor?

mental anchor is anything that brings you back to a state of safety and calm, even when fear or depression is raging inside you.

It doesn't stop the storm—it keeps you from being swept away.

Anchors can be:

* **Physical objects** – a stone, a bracelet, a photo.

* **Sensory experiences** – a scent, a song, a warm drink.

* **Mental images** – a safe place in your mind, a comforting memory.

* **Words** – a mantra, prayer, or affirmation.

Why Anchors Work

When fear or depression hits, your brain's alarm system floods you with stress hormones. Your logical thinking shuts down.

An anchor works by **activating your senses or emotions in a way that signals safety**. This interrupts the panic-depression spiral and helps you regain control.

"You can't calm the storm, so stop trying. What you can do is calm yourself. The storm will pass."* – Timber Hawkeye

Step 1 – Choose Your Anchor

Your anchor should be:

* **Portable** – easy to use anywhere.

* **Personal** – deeply meaningful to you.

* **Positive** – connected to safety, love, or joy.

Examples:

* A smooth pebble from a beach you love.

* A locket with a loved one's photo.

* A scented oil that reminds you of home.

* A short prayer or mantra like *"I am safe right now."*

Step 2 – Charge Your Anchor

Anchors are most powerful when your brain links them to a sense of calm. Here's how to "charge" yours:

1. Sit quietly in a safe, comfortable place.

2. Hold your anchor (or focus on your chosen mantra/scent).

3. Close your eyes and recall a time when you felt safe, happy, or loved.

4. Breathe slowly and deeply, letting the feeling grow.

5. Repeat for 5 minutes, daily, for one week.

This process teaches your brain: *"When I touch/see/smell this, I am safe."*

Step 3 – Use Your Anchor in the Storm

When fear spikes or depression drags you down:

1. Stop whatever you're doing.

2. Grab your anchor.

3. Focus all your attention on it—touch it, look at it, smell it.

4. Breathe slowly, imagining safety flowing back into you.

It's like grabbing onto a rock in the middle of a raging river—you stop getting carried away.

Step 4 – Build Multiple Anchors

One anchor is good. Multiple anchors make you unshakable.

You can create anchors for:

* **Panic attacks** – a specific breathing technique.

* **Sadness** – a playlist of uplifting songs.

* **Loneliness** – a list of friends to call.

The more anchors you have, the faster you can stabilize when the storm hits.

Mini Story: The Teacher and the Bracelet

Meera, a schoolteacher, struggled with panic attacks during class. She was terrified her students would notice.

Her therapist gave her a simple silver bracelet and told her to rub it whenever she felt panic coming. At first, she didn't believe it would help. But after weeks of charging the bracelet with calm, it became her lifeline.

One day, a panic attack started in the middle of a lesson. She quietly touched the bracelet under her desk, breathed slowly, and within minutes, her heartbeat steadied. The storm passed, and she kept teaching.

Practical Exercises for Chapter 3

Exercise 1 – Create Your First Anchor

1. Choose a small object, scent, or phrase that makes you feel safe.

2. Charge it for 5 minutes daily for one week.

3. Use it whenever you feel fear or depression rising.

Exercise 2 – The Safe Place Visualization

1. Close your eyes and imagine a place where you feel completely safe.

2. Picture every detail—colors, sounds, smells.

3. Visit this place in your mind whenever you feel unsteady.

Exercise 3 – Anchor List

Write down 5 anchors you could use in different situations:

* For anxiety in public.

* For sadness at home.

* For panic before sleep.

* For sudden bad news.

* For overwhelming work stress.

Exercise 4 – Anchor + Breath Combo

When using your anchor, pair it with slow breathing (inhale for 4, exhale for 6). This doubles its calming power.

Key Lessons from This Chapter

* Fear and depression are storms; anchors keep you steady until they pass.

* An anchor can be physical, sensory, mental, or verbal.

* Charging your anchor links it to safety in your brain.

* Having multiple anchors makes you stronger in any storm.

In the next chapter**, we'll take on one of the biggest enemies of freedom—**your inner critic**—and learn how to silence it and unleash your inner coach instead.

Chapter 4

Silence the Inner Critic, Unleash the Inner Coach

"Talk to yourself like you would to someone you love." – Brené Brown

****The Voice That Never Sleeps****

If fear and depression are the guards of your invisible prison, the **inner critic** is the warden.

It doesn't just keep you trapped—it convinces you you deserve to be there.

The inner critic is that voice inside your head that says:

* "You're not good enough."

* "You'll fail again."

* "Who do you think you are to try?"

It's a voice that never sleeps, always ready to remind you of your mistakes, weaknesses, and failures—real or imagined.

Over time, if you listen to it long enough, you start believing it's the truth.

Mini Story: The Girl Who Couldn't Win

Priya was talented, creative, and hard-working. Yet, no matter what she achieved—a promotion at work, a compliment from a friend—her first thought was, *"I don't deserve this."*

She had an inner critic so loud that every success felt like a fluke, every mistake like a disaster.

One day, her mentor asked her, *"If someone spoke to your best friend the way you speak to yourself, would you allow it?"*

The question shook her. She realized she had been her own bully for years.

That was the day she decided to learn a new way of talking to herself.

Where the Inner Critic Comes From

Your inner critic is not born with you—it's built over time.

It comes from:

* **Critical parents or teachers** – people who shamed or compared you.

* **Past failures** – moments you felt humiliated or judged.

* **Perfectionism** – the belief that only flawless people are worthy.

* **Fear of rejection** – thinking if you criticize yourself first, others can't hurt you.

Ironically, the inner critic often believes it's helping you—by "protecting" you from failure or embarrassment. But instead of protecting, it paralyzes.

The Inner Critic's Favorite Lies

1. **"You're not ready."**

Truth: You learn as you go. Nobody ever feels 100% ready.

2. **"You'll fail again."**

Truth: Failure is a teacher, not a life sentence.

3. **"You're not as good as them."**

Truth: Comparison steals your focus from your own path.

4. **"You should be further ahead by now."**

Truth: Everyone's timeline is different. Growth is not a race.

"Don't let the noise of your inner critic drown out the sound of your own heart."– Unknown

Step 1 – Notice the Voice

The first step to silencing your inner critic is **awareness**.

When it speaks, notice:

* The words it uses.

* The tone—angry, mocking, disappointed.

* The situations where it shows up most.

Write these down. Awareness weakens its power.

Step 2 – Give It a Name

Just like fear and depression, naming your inner critic helps separate it from you.

Examples:

* "The Judge"

* "The Nag"

* "The Shadow"

Once named, you can say, *"Thanks for your opinion, Judge, but I'm moving forward anyway."*

Step 3 – Challenge Its Lies

When the critic speaks, ask:

* "Is this fact or opinion?"

* "Would I say this to a loved one?"

* "What is a kinder, more helpful truth?"

For example:

Critic: *"You're useless."*

You: *"I'm learning, and I've already made progress."*

Step 4 – Find Your Inner Coach

Your inner coach is the opposite of the critic.

It's the voice that says:

* "You can do this."

* "Mistakes are part of the process."

* "Keep going—you're stronger than you think."

This voice exists in you already. You've used it when encouraging a friend or comforting a child. Now, you'll use it on yourself.

Step 5 – Train the Coach Daily

1. **Morning Pep Talk** – Start each day by saying out loud:

   "Today, I choose to be on my own side."

2. **Affirmations** – Write and repeat statements like:

   * "I am capable and growing."

   * "My best is enough."

3. **Celebrate Small Wins** – Even finishing a chore counts. Recognition strengthens your coach's voice.

Mini Story: The Runner Who Believed Again

Arun loved running, but after an injury, he lost confidence. Every time he tried again, his critic whispered, *"You'll get hurt. You're too slow."*

His therapist told him to imagine running with a supportive friend beside him, speaking encouragement.

He practiced this mental image daily. Slowly, the critic's voice faded, and the coach's voice grew louder. Within months, Arun completed a 5K run—and enjoyed every step.

Practical Exercises for Chapter 4

Exercise 1 – Critic Awareness Journal

For one week, write down:

* What your critic said.

* When it happened.

* How you felt.

Exercise 2 – Name and Talk Back

Give your critic a name. When it speaks, say:

"Thanks, \[Name], but I'm choosing a kinder truth."

Exercise 3 – Build Your Coach's Script

Write down 5 encouraging phrases you can say to yourself daily. Example:

* "I've handled hard things before."

* "This is temporary."

Exercise 4 – The 2-Minute Self-Compassion Break

Place your hand over your heart, close your eyes, and say:

* "This is a hard moment."

* "Hard moments happen to everyone."

* "May I be kind to myself right now."

Key Lessons from This Chapter

* Your inner critic is learned—it can be unlearned.

* Naming and challenging it reduces its control.

* Your inner coach already exists—train it daily.

* Encouragement is not weakness; it's fuel for progress.

In the next chapter, we'll discover *Gratitude as a Weapon Against Darkness*—how shifting focus to what's good can weaken fear and depression's grip on your mind.

Chapter 5

Gratitude as a Weapon Against Darkness

"Gratitude turns what we have into enough." – Melody Beattie

When the Mind Sees Only Shadows

Fear and depression have a way of narrowing your vision.

They take your mind's flashlight and point it only at what's wrong, missing, or frightening in your life.

When you wake up, the first thought is, *"I can't do this."*

When something goes well, the critic says, *"It's not enough."*

When you think about the future, you only see more pain.

This is how fear and depression feed themselves—by training you to focus on the darkness.

But there is a way to fight back.

It's not by ignoring your struggles.

It's by **shifting the light**.

And the most powerful way to do that is with gratitude.

Mini Story: The Man Who Found Light in Prison

Vikram was serving a long prison sentence. At first, he was consumed by anger, regret, and hopelessness. But one day, a volunteer taught him a simple gratitude practice:

"Every night, write down three things you're thankful for, no matter how small."

At first, Vikram thought it was ridiculous. What could he possibly be grateful for in a cell? But he started anyway:

* "The warm sunlight through my window."

* “A letter from my sister.”

* “The taste of hot tea this morning.”

Within months, something shifted. His circumstances hadn’t changed, but his mind had. He began to see beauty in moments he once ignored. He said later:

"Gratitude didn’t open the prison door. But it opened the prison in my mind."

Why Gratitude Works on the Brain

Gratitude is more than just “being thankful.”

It’s a deliberate choice to notice the good in the middle of the bad.

Science shows that gratitude:

* **Releases dopamine and serotonin** – the brain’s natural “feel good” chemicals.

* **Reduces the stress response** – lowering anxiety and fear signals.

* **Builds resilience** – making it easier to bounce back from challenges.

In short, gratitude is not just a nice habit—it's a **mental weapon** against the darkness.

***"It is not joy that makes us grateful, it is gratitude that makes us joyful."* – Brother David Steindl-Rast**

The Resistance to Gratitude

When you're depressed, gratitude can feel fake. You might think:

* "I can't be grateful when my life is falling apart."

* "This is just lying to myself."

But gratitude doesn't deny pain.

It simply says: *"Pain is not the whole story."*

Step 1 – Start Small

Don't pressure yourself to feel thankful for big, abstract things like "life" or "the universe." Start with concrete, simple things:

* The taste of your morning coffee.

* A kind text from a friend.

* A moment of laughter.

Step 2 – Make It a Daily Ritual

Gratitude works best when it's consistent. Pick a time—morning or night—and list 3 things you're grateful for.

Even on bad days, find something. Some days, your list might just be:

* "I'm breathing."

* "I have a roof over my head."

* "This day is over."

That's okay. You're still training your mind to find light.

Step 3 – Feel It, Don't Just List It

Simply writing things down is good, but **feeling** gratitude is where the real power lies.

When you write “I’m grateful for my friend,” pause and picture them. Hear their laugh. Feel the warmth of their presence. Let it sink in for 10 seconds.

This emotional connection rewires your brain faster.

Step 4 – Gratitude in the Moment

Don’t wait for your journal—practice gratitude in real time.

* When you drink water, think, *“This is refreshing.”*

* When you see the sunrise, think, *“This is beautiful.”*

* When someone smiles at you, think, *“That was kind.”*

Over time, this turns into a habit, and you’ll catch yourself feeling thankful without even trying.

Mini Story: The Widow and the Garden

After losing her husband, Leela fell into deep depression. She couldn't imagine ever feeling joy again.

One day, she noticed a single flower blooming in her neglected garden. For the first time in months, she felt a spark of warmth.

She decided to look for one beautiful thing each day—just one.

Some days, it was a bird's song. Other days, the smell of rain.

Years later, she said, *"I didn't heal overnight. But those little moments of gratitude were stepping stones back to life."*

Practical Exercises for Chapter 5

Exercise 1 – The Gratitude Journal

Every day, write down 3 things you're grateful for. Feel each one for 10 seconds.

Exercise 2 – Gratitude Snapshot

Set an alarm on your phone 3 times a day. When it rings, pause and notice something you're grateful for in that exact moment.

Exercise 3 – Gratitude Letter

Write a letter to someone who has helped you. You don't have to send it, but if you do, it can be life-changing for both of you.

Exercise 4 – Gratitude Before Sleep

As you lie in bed, think of one good thing from the day—even if it's tiny. Let it be the last thought before you sleep.

Key Lessons from This Chapter

* Gratitude shifts your mind's focus from darkness to light.

* It works on the brain like a natural antidepressant.

* Start small, be consistent, and connect emotionally.

* Even in hard times, there is always *something* to be grateful for.

In the next chapter, we'll face fear head-on with *The Fear Ladder*—a proven way to turn panic into power by conquering challenges one step at a time.

Chapter 6

The Fear Ladder: Turning Panic into Power

"Do the thing you fear, and the death of fear is certain." – Ralph Waldo Emerson

Why Fear Feels Like a Wall

When fear controls your life, it feels like you're standing in front of a giant wall.

It's so high you can't climb it, so wide you can't go around it, and so solid you can't break through it.

So you do what feels safe—you turn away.

But each time you avoid it, the wall seems to grow taller.

Fear feeds on avoidance. The more you run, the stronger it becomes.

But here's the truth:

Fear is not a wall—it's a ladder you haven't started climbing yet.

Mini Story: The Man Who Feared Bridges

Amit loved traveling, but he had one problem—he was terrified of crossing bridges. Even the thought made his hands sweat. He avoided trips that involved bridges, even if it meant missing out on adventures with friends.

One day, his therapist drew a ladder on a piece of paper.

"Your fear is at the top," she said. "We don't have to jump there. We just take one step at a time."

Amit's "Fear Ladder" looked like this:

1. Look at pictures of bridges.

2. Watch videos of people crossing bridges.

3. Stand near a small footbridge without crossing.

4. Walk halfway across a short bridge with a friend.

5. Walk fully across a small bridge.

6. Cross a bigger bridge.

7. Drive over a long bridge.

Within six months, Amit was crossing bridges without panic.

The Fear Ladder Explained

The **Fear Ladder** is a method where you break your fear into small, manageable steps and face them gradually.

Instead of forcing yourself to tackle your biggest fear all at once (which can overwhelm you), you **desensitize** your brain to fear little by little.

This works because:

* It gives your brain proof that nothing terrible happens.

* It rewires your nervous system to stay calm in situations that once triggered panic.

* It builds confidence with every step.

"The journey of a thousand miles begins with a single step." – Lao Tzu

Step 1 – Identify Your Fear

Write down one fear that limits your life.

Examples:

* Public speaking

* Social situations

* Driving

* Heights

* Crowds

Choose a fear that, if reduced, would improve your quality of life.

Step 2 – Break It into Steps

Divide the fear into 5–10 smaller challenges, starting from the least scary to the most.

Example: **Fear of Public Speaking**

1. Speak in front of a mirror for 1 minute.

2. Record yourself speaking and watch it.

3. Practice in front of one friend.

4. Share a story at a small group meeting.

5. Give a 5-minute talk to a familiar group.

6. Speak to a small audience of strangers.

7. Give a presentation to a larger audience.

Step 3 – Face the First Step Until It's Comfortable

Don't rush up the ladder. Stay on the first step until your anxiety level drops significantly. This may take hours, days, or weeks—progress is what matters, not speed.

Step 4 – Move to the Next Step

Once you feel calm at one level, move up. You may still feel nervous, but it will be less intense. Over time, the fear will lose its grip.

Step 5 – Celebrate Every Victory

Each time you climb a rung, write it down or reward yourself. Small celebrations make your brain associate courage with pleasure, reinforcing progress.

Mini Story: The Woman Who Feared Socializing

Rina had social anxiety so strong that she avoided all parties. Her fear ladder looked like this:

1. Make eye contact with a stranger.

2. Smile at a cashier.

3. Say “hello” to a neighbor.

4. Ask someone for the time.

5. Have a 1-minute conversation with a stranger.

6. Attend a small social gathering.

7. Go to a larger party for 30 minutes.

A year later, she wasn’t just attending parties—she was enjoying them.

Overcoming Fear Setbacks

Fear reduction isn’t always a straight climb. Some days you may slip down a rung—and that’s okay.

Tips for setbacks:

* **Be kind to yourself** – Courage isn’t about never slipping, it’s about climbing again.

* **Review your wins** – Look back at how far you’ve come.

* **Stay consistent** – Even 5 minutes of practice keeps progress alive.

Practical Exercises for Chapter 6

Exercise 1 – Build Your Fear Ladder

1. Choose one fear.

2. Write 5–10 steps from easiest to hardest.

3. Commit to practicing the first step this week.

Exercise 2 – The 0–10 Fear Scale

Before and after each step, rate your fear from 0 (calm) to 10 (panic). Over time, you'll see the numbers drop.

Exercise 3 – Courage Log

Keep a notebook where you record:

* The step you took.

* How you felt before, during, and after.

* What you learned.

Exercise 4 – Reward System

Decide on small rewards for completing steps—like a favorite snack, watching a movie, or buying yourself something small.

Key Lessons from This Chapter

* Fear grows with avoidance but shrinks with gradual exposure.

* The Fear Ladder turns overwhelming challenges into manageable steps.

* Progress is more important than speed—climbing slowly is still climbing.

* Celebrating each rung builds motivation and rewires your brain for courage.

In the next chapter, we'll explore *Movement and the Mind*—how physical activity can lift depression, calm fear, and reset your emotional balance.

Chapter 7

Movement and the Mind: How Motion Heals Emotion

"You can't think your way out of a dark place. Sometimes, you have to move your way out." – 0Unknown

When the Body Stays Still, the Mind Stays Stuck

When fear and depression take hold, the body slows down.

You might stay in bed longer, avoid leaving the house, or sit for hours lost in thought.

It feels safe to be still—but stillness can become a trap.

The less you move, the more your mood sinks. The more your mood sinks, the less you want to move.

But here's the truth: **Motion changes emotion.**

Mini Story: The Walk That Saved Him

Arun was in the middle of the worst depression of his life. He hadn't left his apartment in days. His therapist didn't tell him to "think positive" or "try harder." She said only one thing:

"Walk for five minutes."

The first day, he dragged himself outside and walked around the block. It didn't cure him. But the next day, he walked for seven minutes. Then ten.

By week three, he was walking thirty minutes a day. His sleep improved. His energy returned. And slowly, his mind began to clear.

Why Movement Works on the Brain

Movement doesn't just make your body stronger—it rewires your brain chemistry:

* **Releases endorphins** – natural mood lifters.

* **Reduces cortisol** – lowering stress and fear signals.

* **Boosts serotonin and dopamine** – stabilizing mood and motivation.

* **Improves brain plasticity** – making it easier to learn new habits.

Even light movement—like stretching or slow walking—can shift your mental state.

***"The mind is the body's servant. What you do with the body will directly affect the mind."* – Unknown**

Step 1 – Start Small and Specific

Don't aim for an intense workout on day one. If you're depressed or anxious, your body needs **gentle, consistent** movement.

Examples:

* 3 minutes of stretching after waking up.

* Walking to the end of the street.

* Dancing to one song.

The goal is not fitness—it's breaking the cycle of stillness.

Step 2 – Make It Daily

Consistency matters more than intensity. Even if you only move for 5 minutes, doing it daily builds a habit that your brain starts craving.

Step 3 – Choose Joyful Movement

You don't have to run marathons. Choose activities that feel enjoyable or at least tolerable:

* Walking in nature

* Cycling slowly

* Gentle yoga

* Swimming

* Playing a sport you love

* Dancing in your living room

Step 4 – Pair Movement with Mindfulness

While you move, notice:

* The rhythm of your breath.

* The feeling of your feet touching the ground.

* The sounds and sights around you.

Mindful movement doubles the mental health benefits by grounding you in the present moment.

Mini Story: The Woman Who Danced Again

After a painful breakup, Kavita lost all motivation. She remembered that she once loved dancing, so she made herself dance for just one song every morning.

Some days she cried while dancing. Other days she laughed. But she kept going.

Months later, she joined a dance class, met new friends, and said:

"The dance didn’t just move my body—it moved my heart back to life."

Step 5 – Use the “Movement Ladder”

If your energy is very low, build it up like a Fear Ladder:

1. Stretch for 2 minutes in bed.

2. Stand up and walk in place for 1 minute.

3. Walk around your home.

4. Walk outside for 5 minutes.

5. Increase to 10–15 minutes.

Progress is progress, no matter how small.

Practical Exercises for Chapter 7

Exercise 1 – 5-Minute Morning Move

Right after waking, do 5 minutes of any movement—stretching, walking, or dancing.

Exercise 2 – Movement Log

Each day, record:

* How long you moved.

* What you did.

* How you felt before and after.

Exercise 3 – Joy List

Write 5 movements you enjoy or want to try. Pick one daily.

Exercise 4 – Nature Walk Challenge

Once a week, walk in a natural setting—park, garden, or near water. Nature enhances the calming effects of movement.

Key Lessons from This Chapter

* Motion changes emotion—movement is a direct path out of mental stagnation.

* Start small, be consistent, and choose joyful activities.

* Mindful movement grounds you in the present and reduces anxiety.

* Progress is measured in steps taken, not speed or distance.

In the next chapter, we'll unlock *The Power of Connection*—how relationships can be a lifeline out of fear and depression, and how to rebuild trust in others when you feel safest alone.

Chapter 8

The Power of Connection: Relationships as Lifelines

"We don't heal in isolation, but in community."
– S. Kelley Harrell

The Loneliness Trap

Fear and depression whisper the same dangerous lie: *"You're better off alone."*

You start avoiding calls. You stop replying to messages. You make excuses to stay home.

It feels safe at first. No one can judge you. No one can hurt you. But isolation feeds the darkness—until you're left in a quiet room where your thoughts become your loudest, cruelest companions.

Humans were not built to heal alone. Connection is not a luxury; it's a lifeline.

Mini Story: The Woman Who Stopped Answering the Phone

Saira used to be the life of every gathering. But when depression hit, she withdrew completely.

One day, an old friend knocked on her door and said, *"I'm not here to fix you. I'm just here so you're not alone."*

That one act of kindness became the first thread pulling Saira back to life. She started answering one call a week. Then one coffee a month. Eventually, she rejoined her book club.

"It wasn't therapy that saved me first—it was people who didn't give up on me."

Why Connection Heals the Mind

Science shows that healthy relationships:

* **Reduce cortisol** – lowering stress and fear signals.

* **Boost oxytocin** – the "bonding hormone" that promotes trust and calm.

* **Provide perspective** – helping you see beyond your own thoughts.

* **Increase accountability** – making you more likely to take positive action.

***"A shared joy is a double joy; a shared sorrow is half a sorrow."* – Swedish Proverb**

Step 1 – Identify Your Relationship Circle

Draw three circles:

* **Inner Circle** – people you trust completely (close friends, family).

* **Middle Circle** – friendly but less intimate connections (colleagues, neighbors).

* **Outer Circle** – acquaintances, online groups, community members.

This helps you see where support can come from—and where to focus energy.

Step 2 – Reconnect, One Step at a Time

If you've been isolated, jumping straight into big social events can be overwhelming. Start small:

* Reply to one message today.

* Call one person this week.

* Meet someone for coffee this month.

These small steps reopen the door without forcing you into uncomfortable situations.

Step 3 – Choose Nourishing Relationships

Not all relationships are healing. Some drain your energy, increase fear, or make depression worse.

Ask yourself:

* Do I feel safe with this person?

* Do I feel seen and heard?

* Do I feel better or worse after spending time with them?

Focus on people who lift you up, not pull you down.

Step 4 – Be Honest About Your Struggles

True connection is built on authenticity. You don't have to share every detail, but saying, *"I've been going through a hard time"* can open the door to deeper support.

Often, you'll discover others are struggling too—and connection grows through mutual understanding.

Mini Story: The Men's Group That Changed Everything

Ravi joined a local men's group reluctantly, thinking it would be awkward. But within minutes, he heard another man describe feelings of anxiety and hopelessness that mirrored his own.

For the first time, Ravi realized he wasn't broken—he was human. The group became his safe space, and in time, his fear of judgment faded.

Step 5 – Give as Well as Receive

Helping others can be a powerful antidepressant. It shifts your focus from your own pain to making a difference, no matter how small.

Ways to give:

* Listen without judgment.

* Offer practical help.

* Volunteer in your community.

When you contribute, you strengthen your own sense of purpose and belonging.

Practical Exercises for Chapter 8

Exercise 1 – Connection Audit

Write down 5 people in your life and rate how each interaction makes you feel. Focus on nurturing the ones that energize you.

Exercise 2 – One Message a Day

Send one kind message daily—for a week—to a friend, family member, or acquaintance. It can be as simple as, *"Thinking of you today."*

Exercise 3 – The Listening Challenge

In your next conversation, spend more time listening than speaking. Connection deepens when people feel heard.

Exercise 4 – Join One Group

Find a local club, class, or online community that interests you. Commit to showing up at least twice.

Key Lessons from This Chapter

* Isolation strengthens fear and depression—connection weakens them.

* Start with small, safe steps toward reconnection.

* Focus on relationships that nourish, not drain, your energy.

* Giving to others boosts your own healing.

In the next chapter, we'll explore *The Warrior's Mindset*—how to develop unshakable resilience so fear and depression can knock you down, but never keep you there.

Chapter 9

The Warrior's Mindset: Resilience Over Perfection

"Fall seven times and stand up eight."* – Japanese Proverb

Why Life Doesn't Reward Perfection

Fear and depression often convince you that you have to be flawless before you try, that mistakes mean failure, and failure means you're worthless.

This thinking keeps you frozen.

But here's the truth: **Life doesn't reward perfection—it rewards persistence.**

Warriors aren't people who never get hurt. They're people who get knocked down and still rise.

Resilience—not perfection—is the ultimate weapon against fear and depression.

Mini Story: The Boxer Who Never Quit

Arjun was a young boxer who lost his first three matches. Each defeat bruised not only his body but his pride. His friends told him to quit.

His coach told him something different:

"You're not here to win every round. You're here to learn how to take a hit and keep fighting."

Arjun trained harder. He lost again. And again. But he kept showing up. Eventually, he won.

Not because he was perfect—but because he refused to stop.

The Truth About Resilience

Resilience is not about ignoring pain or pretending everything is fine. It's about:

* Bouncing back after setbacks.

* Adapting when life changes unexpectedly.

* Continuing despite fear, doubt, or discomfort.

You can train resilience just like you train a muscle—through challenge, recovery, and repetition.

***"A smooth sea never made a skilled sailor."* – Franklin D. Roosevelt**

Step 1 – Accept That Setbacks Are Part of the Journey

The most resilient people understand that failure, rejection, and mistakes are inevitable. Instead of seeing them as the end, they see them as feedback.

Ask yourself:

* “What is this teaching me?”

* “How can I adapt?”

Step 2 – Shift from Victim to Warrior

Fear and depression can make you feel powerless—a victim of life’s circumstances.

The warrior mindset says:

* “This happened, and it’s hard—but I still have choices.”

* “I can’t control everything, but I can control my next step.”

Step 3 – Train in Discomfort

Warriors don’t wait until life is easy to act—they practice discomfort on purpose.

Ways to train:

* Take a cold shower.

* Speak up in a meeting.

* Try something new where you might fail.

Small acts of voluntary discomfort prepare you for the involuntary challenges life throws at you.

Step 4 – Build Recovery Rituals

Resilience is not just about pushing—it’s about resting, recharging, and rebuilding.

Your recovery rituals might include:

* Sleep

* Meditation

* Journaling

* Time in nature

* Laughter with friends

A burned-out warrior is no warrior at all.

Mini Story: The Single Mother Who Kept Going

Meena's husband left when her child was two. She had no job, no savings, and no idea what to do next.

She cried. She panicked. But the next morning, she started making phone calls. She applied for jobs. She learned new skills.

Years later, she said:

"I didn't feel strong every day. But I acted like I was—and strength caught up with me."

Step 5 – Celebrate Effort, Not Just Outcome

Resilient people focus on showing up, not just winning.

Every time you act despite fear, you train your brain to see yourself as capable.

Write down your small wins. Remind yourself that consistency is courage in disguise.

Practical Exercises for Chapter 9

Exercise 1 – Setback Reframe

Think of a past setback. Write down three lessons or strengths you gained from it.

Exercise 2 – Discomfort Practice

Choose one small act of discomfort to do daily for a week. Record how you feel afterward.

Exercise 3 – Warrior Journal

Each night, write one thing you faced today, even if it scared you.

Exercise 4 – Effort Tracker

Create a checklist of actions (not results) that move you toward your goals. Reward yourself for completing them.

Key Lessons from This Chapter

* Perfection is an illusion—resilience is real power.

* Setbacks are feedback, not proof of failure.

* Training in discomfort prepares you for life's storms.

* Recovery is as essential as persistence.

In the next chapter, we'll explore The Power of Self-Compassion: Being on Your Own Side

Chapter 11

The Power of Self-Compassion: Being on Your Own Side

"You've been criticizing yourself for years and it hasn't worked. Try approving of yourself and see what happens." – Louise Hay

Why Self-Compassion Matters

Fear and depression often come with a cruel companion: *self-criticism*.

That voice in your head that says:

* "I'm weak."

* "I always mess things up."

* "I don't deserve happiness."

It's exhausting, isn't it?

It's like fighting a battle every day—and realizing the enemy lives inside your own mind.

But here's the breakthrough: **You don't have to keep fighting yourself.**

When you learn to treat yourself with kindness instead of cruelty, healing accelerates.

Self-compassion is not self-pity. It's not laziness. It's not selfish.

It's simply deciding to be on your own side.

Mini Story: The Burned-Out Student

Ritika was a hardworking university student. But after failing an exam, her self-talk turned vicious:

"You're stupid. You'll never succeed. You're a failure."

Her depression worsened. She isolated herself. She wanted to quit.

Her counselor asked her a question:

"If your best friend failed, would you say those same words to her?"

Ritika shook her head. *"Of course not. I'd tell her it's just one test, that she's smart, that she'll do better next time."*

The counselor said: *"Then why not treat yourself the same way?"*

That was her turning point. Ritika began practicing self-compassion. Slowly, her inner enemy transformed into an ally.

The Myths of Self-Compassion

Many people resist self-compassion because they misunderstand it. Let's clear up the myths:

* **Myth 1:** "Self-compassion makes you weak."

Truth: It makes you stronger—because you stop wasting energy beating yourself up.

* **Myth 2:** "It means making excuses."

Truth: Compassion isn't about ignoring mistakes—it's about encouraging yourself to learn from them.

* **Myth 3:** "It's selfish."

Truth: When you treat yourself well, you have more energy and kindness to give to others.

"Talk to yourself like you would to someone you love." – Brené Brown

The Three Parts of Self-Compassion

Psychologist Kristin Neff describes three pillars of self-compassion:

1. **Self-Kindness instead of Self-Judgment**

– Speak to yourself with encouragement, not criticism.

– Replace “I’m worthless” with “I’m struggling, but I’m trying.”

2. **Common Humanity instead of Isolation**

– Remember: everyone fails, everyone struggles. You are not alone.

3. **Mindfulness instead of Over-Identification**

– Notice your pain without drowning in it. Say, *"This is hard,"* instead of *"This is who I am forever."*

Step 1 – Notice the Voice

The first step is awareness. Begin to pay attention to how you talk to yourself.

Would you speak to a child that way? A friend? A loved one?

If not, it's time to change the voice.

Step 2 – Flip the Script

When you hear harsh self-talk, pause and ask:

* *"What would I say to a friend right now?"*

* *"What's a kinder way to see this?"*

Example:

* Harsh voice: "I failed again. I'm hopeless."

* Compassionate voice: "I failed this time, but failure is how we learn. I can try again."

Step 3 – Small Acts of Kindness Toward Yourself

Self-compassion is not only about words—it's also about actions.

* Rest when your body is tired.

* Eat nourishing food.

* Allow yourself to enjoy small pleasures without guilt.

Every act of kindness tells your mind: *"I am worth caring for."*

Mini Story: The Mirror Exercise

Rahul was struggling with deep self-hatred. His therapist gave him a simple daily assignment:

Look in the mirror every morning and say, *"I'm learning to be on my own side."*

At first, he felt ridiculous. But over time, he began to believe it. Months later, Rahul said, *"The mirror became my ally, not my enemy."*

Practical Exercises for Chapter 11

Exercise 1 – Letter to Yourself

Write a letter to yourself as if you were comforting a close friend who is going through the same struggle. Keep it gentle, kind, and encouraging.

Exercise 2 – The Kindness Pause

Whenever you catch your inner critic, place your hand on your chest, take a deep breath, and say one kind sentence to yourself (e.g., *"I'm doing my best."*).

Exercise 3 – Replace One Criticism a Day

Write down one negative self-thought you have each day. Then rewrite it into a compassionate version.

Exercise 4 – Self-Care Commitment

List three small daily acts of kindness you can give yourself (like resting, drinking water, or listening to music). Commit to them for a week.

Key Lessons from This Chapter

* Self-criticism fuels fear and depression—self-compassion weakens them.

* Being kind to yourself doesn't make you lazy; it makes you stronger.

* Everyone struggles—your pain is part of the human story, not a personal flaw.

* You can re-train your inner voice into one of kindness, encouragement, and love.

In the next chapter, we'll explore *Rewriting Your Inner Story*—how to change the hidden script that shapes your identity and future.

Chapter 12

Rewriting Your Inner Story: Changing the Script of Your Life

"The story you tell yourself is the story you live." – Brené Brown

The Hidden Script Running Your Life

Every life is guided by an invisible script.

It’s the collection of beliefs you hold about yourself:

* “I’m not good enough.”

* “I always fail.”

* “Nothing ever works out for me.”

Most of these stories aren’t even yours. They were planted in you by parents, teachers, bullies, culture, or painful experiences. Yet, without realizing it, you live as if they are absolute truth.

But here's the breakthrough: **You are the author. You can rewrite the story.**

Mini Story: The Boy Called 'Stupid'

When Aman was in school, a teacher once called him *"stupid"* in front of the class.

That one word dug deep. For years, Aman told himself, *"I'm not smart enough. I can't achieve big things."*

His grades, his career choices, even his relationships—all were shaped by that script.

At 30, a mentor asked him: *"Who told you you're stupid? And why are you still believing them?"*

It hit Aman like lightning. He realized he was living someone else's story. That day, he began to rewrite it.

Years later, Aman runs a successful business. His story is no longer *"I'm stupid."* It's *"I'm a lifelong learner who grows every day."*

The Power of Narrative

Your mind is a storyteller. It takes scattered events and strings them into meaning.

That meaning becomes your identity.

But identities are not fixed. They're just repeated stories.

Change the story, and you change the life.

***"The most powerful stories are the ones we tell ourselves about ourselves."* – Unknown**

Step 1 – Identify Your Old Script

Start by listening carefully to your self-talk.

Write down recurring negative thoughts like:

* "I'm unlucky."

* "I always ruin things."

* "No one cares about me."

These are not facts—they are scripts. And scripts can be edited.

Step 2 – Challenge the Script

Ask yourself:

* Is this absolutely true?

* Where did I first learn this?

* If a friend told me this about themselves, what would I say?

Often, you'll discover the script has holes, exaggerations, or outright lies.

Step 3 – Write the New Story

Replace the old script with an empowering one.

Examples:

* Old: "I'm unlucky." → New: "I create my own opportunities."

* Old: "I always fail." → New: "Every setback is training for my success."

* Old: "No one cares about me." → New: "I am learning to surround myself with people who value me."

Mini Story: The Woman Who Rewrote Her Childhood

Priya grew up in a broken home where she was often ignored. She carried the script: *"I'm unlovable."*

In therapy, she rewrote it: *"I survived neglect. That makes me strong. I am worthy of love and will build it for myself."*

That shift changed everything. She attracted healthier friendships, pursued her passions, and even started a support group for women with similar backgrounds.

Her old story was pain. Her new story was power.

Step 4 – Reinforce the New Story

A story isn't rewritten in a single day. You must repeat it until it becomes your default.

Ways to reinforce:

* Daily affirmations.

* Journaling the new narrative.

* Sharing your new story with others.

* Acting as if the story is already true.

***"Don't be satisfied with stories. Unfold your own myth."* – Rumi**

Step 5 – Live Into the New Identity

The most powerful way to lock in a new story is through action.

If your new story is *"I am brave,"* do small brave things.

If your new story is *"I am worthy,"* treat yourself with dignity.

Each action is like writing another page in your book.

Practical Exercises for Chapter 12

Exercise 1 – Life Chapters

Write your life as three chapters:

* Past: What script shaped me?

* Present: What script am I living now?

* Future: What script do I choose to live next?

Exercise 2 – Flip the Script

Take one negative belief and rewrite it into a positive, empowering one. Repeat this daily for a week.

Exercise 3 – Affirmation Recording

Record yourself reading your new story aloud. Listen to it every morning.

Exercise 4 – Act As If

Choose one small daily action that proves your new story is true. (If your story is *"I am confident,"* speak up once a day.)

Key Lessons from This Chapter

* Your inner story shapes your reality more than external events.

* Old scripts come from the past, but they don't have to define the future.

* Rewriting your story involves noticing, challenging, and replacing negative narratives.

* Action is the ink that writes the new story into permanence.

In the next chapter, we'll explore *Mindfulness in Motion*—how to anchor yourself in the present moment and find calm even in the middle of chaos.

Chapter 13

Mindfulness in Motion: Finding Calm in the Present

"The present moment is the only place where life exists."* – Thich Nhat Hanh

**Why the Present Moment Matters**

Fear lives in the future: *"What if this goes wrong?"*

Depression lives in the past: *"I should have done better."*

But life itself? It lives here—in the present.

The only moment you can breathe, act, heal, or enjoy is *now*.

When you learn to anchor yourself in the present, you break free from the endless replay of regrets and the constant worry of “what if.” That’s where **mindfulness in motion** becomes a life-changing practice.

Mini Story: The Man Who Walked Off His Panic

Vikram suffered from severe panic attacks. He often felt trapped, his heart racing, his mind screaming. One therapist told him:

"Don’t fight the panic—walk with it."

So the next time a panic attack began, he went outside and started walking. Step by step, he focused on his breathing, his feet touching the ground, the rhythm of his body.

The panic didn’t vanish instantly, but it lost its grip. For the first time, Vikram felt he had a tool to meet fear in the moment.

That simple act of mindful walking became his daily medicine.

What Is Mindfulness in Motion?

Mindfulness in motion means combining awareness with activity. Instead of escaping into thoughts while moving, you bring your full attention to what your body is doing.

Examples:

* Walking with awareness.

* Stretching or yoga with attention to breath.

* Washing dishes while noticing the warm water and soap.

* Eating slowly, savoring each bite.

It's about turning ordinary activities into grounding practices.

***"Wherever you are, be there totally."* – Eckhart Tolle**

Step 1 – Slow Down

Fear and depression often rush or paralyze you.

Mindfulness invites you to slow down enough to notice:

* The texture of your food.

* The sensation of your breath.

* The sound of birds outside.

Slowing down turns life from a blur into a blessing.

Step 2 – Engage the Senses

The senses anchor you to the present.

When your mind drifts, use the **5-4-3-2-1 method**:

* 5 things you can see.

* 4 things you can touch.

* 3 things you can hear.

* 2 things you can smell.

* 1 thing you can taste.

This simple act pulls your attention out of fear or sadness and into now.

Step 3 – Breathe With Movement

Your breath is always with you—and it can be your anchor.

Try this during a walk:

* Inhale for 3 steps.

* Exhale for 3 steps.

Repeat.

Suddenly, walking becomes a moving meditation.

**Mini Story: The Mother Who Found Peace in Chores**

Shalini, a mother of two, used to resent household chores. She felt trapped in an endless cycle of cleaning and cooking. Her anxiety worsened.

One day she read about mindful living and decided to try it.

While washing dishes, she focused on the warm water, the circular motions, the shine of the plates. Instead of rushing, she breathed and stayed present.

To her surprise, the task became calming.

She said later: *"The dishes became my therapy."*

Step 4 – Move With Gratitude

When you walk, stretch, or exercise, add gratitude. Say silently:

* "Thank you, legs, for carrying me."

* "Thank you, breath, for keeping me alive."

Gratitude turns motion into meditation.

Step 5 – Create Rituals of Presence

Choose 1–2 daily activities and make them mindful rituals. Examples:

* Drinking morning tea with full awareness.

* Taking a slow, mindful walk after dinner.

* Stretching for 5 minutes before bed.

Over time, these rituals create islands of peace in your day.

Practical Exercises for Chapter 13

Exercise 1 – Walking Meditation

Go for a 10-minute walk. Focus on your steps, your breath, and what you see. When your mind drifts, gently bring it back.

Exercise 2 – 5-4-3-2-1 Grounding

Use this whenever anxiety rises. List what you see, touch, hear, smell, taste.

Exercise 3 – Mindful Chores

Pick one daily chore (dishes, sweeping, cooking). Do it slowly and with full awareness.

Exercise 4 – Gratitude in Motion

During any physical activity, thank your body for what it's doing.

Key Lessons from This Chapter

* Fear and depression pull you out of the present—mindfulness pulls you back in.

* You don't need silence or meditation pillows—everyday activities can be mindful.

* The senses and breath are your anchors to now.

* Presence transforms ordinary routines into healing rituals.

In the next chapter, we'll explore *Building Your Safe Haven*—how to design your environment so it supports peace, strength, and recovery.

Chapter 14

Building Your Safe Haven: Creating Environments That Heal

**"Your environment shapes you more than you shape it."* – Unknown*

The Hidden Power of Your Environment

Have you noticed how certain places make you instantly calm, while others make you tense the moment you walk in?

That's no accident.

Your surroundings affect your mood, thoughts, and even your energy.

A cluttered, noisy, or toxic environment can fuel fear and depression.

But a safe, calming space can become your **anchor of healing**.

Your environment is not just where you live—it's the air you breathe, the light you see, the sounds you hear, and the people you let in.

If fear and depression are storms, then your safe haven is your shelter.

Mini Story: The Man Who Created a Peace Corner

Rajesh lived in a chaotic joint family household. He loved his family, but constant noise and conflict drained him. His depression worsened because he never had a space to breathe.

One day, he decided to claim a small corner of his room. He put a chair, a soft cushion, a plant, and a lamp there. He called it his *"peace corner."*

Every evening, he sat there with tea and calming music. Over time, that little space became his sanctuary.

"I couldn't control the whole house," he said, *"but I could control this corner. And that saved me."*

Step 1 – Declutter Your Mind by Decluttering Your Space

Clutter is not just physical—it’s mental. A messy environment keeps your brain in a state of low-grade stress.

Start small:

* Clear your desk.

* Organize one shelf.

* Donate what you don’t need.

Each act of decluttering tells your mind: *“I’m making space for peace.”*

"Outer order contributes to inner calm." – Gretchen Rubin

Step 2 – Add Comfort and Calm

Your space should feel safe, welcoming, and soothing. Ask yourself:

* What colors calm me? (Soft blues, greens, and neutrals often help.)

* What textures comfort me? (A soft blanket, a favorite chair.)

* What sounds ground me? (Nature sounds, soft music, silence.)

Even one or two small changes can transform how you feel.

Step 3 – Invite Nature Inside

Nature heals. Studies show that greenery, sunlight, and fresh air reduce stress and lift mood.

Ways to bring nature into your safe haven:

* A small plant or flower.

* Opening windows for fresh air.

* Natural light whenever possible.

* Photographs of natural scenes if real nature isn't accessible.

Mini Story: The Woman Who Painted Her Walls

Anita struggled with depression during the lockdown. Her dark, dull room felt like a prison. One day, she bought paint and turned her walls a soft sky blue. She hung fairy lights and added two indoor plants.

She said: *"I couldn't change the world outside. But I could change the world inside my room."*

Her mood lifted noticeably. Small changes created big relief.

Step 4 – Build Routines into Your Haven

A safe haven isn't just about objects—it's about what you *do* there.

* Journal in your peace corner.

* Meditate in a specific chair.

* Read a calming book before bed.

Over time, your brain begins to associate that space with safety and calm.

Step 5 – Protect Your Haven

Not everyone deserves access to your healing space.

Set boundaries. If someone's energy drains you, it's okay to limit their presence in your safe haven.

Remember: this is your sanctuary. Protect it like a warrior.

Practical Exercises for Chapter 14

****Exercise 1 – Space Audit****

Walk through your home and note: *What spaces drain me? What spaces lift me?* Write them down.

****Exercise 2 – Create a Peace Corner****

Choose one small spot (a chair, a desk, a corner). Add one object that calms you—a candle, a plant, a soft pillow.

****Exercise 3 – 10-Minute Declutter****

Set a timer and declutter for just 10 minutes daily. Small wins add up.

****Exercise 4 – Ritual of Calm****

Pick one activity (tea, journaling, meditation) and always do it in your safe space. Train your mind to associate the activity with peace.

Key Lessons from This Chapter

* Your environment either fuels stress or fosters peace—choose wisely.

* Decluttering creates mental clarity.

* Adding nature, light, and comfort transforms any space into healing ground.

* Rituals and boundaries turn your environment into a true safe haven.

In the next chapter, we'll explore **The Courage to Let Go: Releasing What No Longer Serves You**

Chapter 15

The Courage to Let Go: Releasing What No Longer Serves You

"Some of us think holding on makes us strong, but sometimes it is letting go."* – Hermann Hesse

The Chains We Carry

Fear and depression often tighten their grip because of what we refuse to release.

We hold on to:

* Past mistakes.

* Old grudges.

* Toxic relationships.

* Regrets about what “should have been.”

We cling, believing that if we just hold tighter, things will change. But the truth is this: **Holding on often keeps us trapped. Letting go is what sets us free.**

Mini Story: The Man Who Held the Rope

A story is told of a man who slipped off a cliff but managed to grab a rope. Hanging there, terrified, he screamed for help. Hours passed. His arms grew weak. Finally, in despair, he let go—only to discover the ground was just two feet below.

Many of us live like that—clinging desperately, when freedom is right beneath us if we have the courage to release.

Why Letting Go Is So Hard

Our minds convince us that letting go means losing. But in reality:

* Letting go of anger gives you peace.

* Letting go of regret gives you freedom.

* Letting go of toxic people gives you space to grow.

* Letting go of perfection gives you joy in progress.

It's not weakness to release—it's wisdom.

***"Holding on is believing that there's only a past; letting go is knowing that there's a future."* – Daphne Rose Kingma**

Step 1 – Identify What You're Holding On To

Take a moment and ask yourself:

* Am I carrying anger toward someone?

* Am I replaying past mistakes?

* Am I staying in a relationship that hurts me?

* Am I clinging to a version of life that no longer exists?

Awareness is the first step toward release.

Step 2 – Understand What It Costs You

Every burden you carry weighs on your mind and body.

Ask: *"What is this costing me in peace, health, and happiness?"*

When you realize the cost, the choice to let go becomes easier.

Step 3 – Forgive, Not Forget

Forgiveness is not saying what happened was okay. It's saying: *"I refuse to let this event control my life anymore."*

When you forgive, you cut the chain between you and the pain.

Mini Story: The Father's Letter

Arun carried deep resentment toward his father, who had abandoned the family. For decades, anger ate at him. One day, his therapist asked him to write a letter—not to send, but to release.

Arun poured out every hurt, every disappointment. Then, at the end, he wrote: *"I release you. I choose peace."*

He cried as he read it aloud. But afterward, he felt lighter, as if years of weight had been lifted. His depression began to ease—not because his father changed, but because *he* did.

Step 4 – Release the Illusion of Control

Much of fear and depression comes from trying to control the uncontrollable. We replay the past, predict the future, and exhaust ourselves with "what if."

Letting go means accepting:

* The past cannot be changed.

* The future cannot be fully controlled.

* The only place of power is here, now.

***"You will find that it is necessary to let things go; simply for the reason that they are heavy."* – C. JoyBell C.**

Step 5 – Create Rituals of Release

Letting go is easier when you ritualize it. Here are powerful ways:

* **The Letting Go Letter** – Write a letter to the person, event, or feeling you're releasing. Then tear it, burn it safely, or bury it.

* **The Box Exercise** – Imagine putting your worries into a box each night and locking it until tomorrow.

* **Breath Release** – With each exhale, visualize releasing pain, guilt, or anger.

Rituals give your mind a physical symbol of freedom.

Mini Story: The Widow and the Box

Meera lost her husband suddenly and carried unbearable grief. Every night, her mind raced with memories, regrets, and guilt. Her counselor gave her a small wooden box and said: *"Each night, write your worries on paper and put them inside. Leave them there until morning."*

At first, she resisted. But slowly, the ritual worked. She slept better. Her grief didn't vanish, but it stopped drowning her.

"The box held my pain so I could rest," she later said.

Step 6 – Fill the Space With Something New

Letting go creates a void. If you don't fill it, old habits return.

Fill your freed space with:

* Joyful activities.

* Healthy relationships.

* Learning and growth.

* Gratitude practices.

Freedom isn't just release—it's renewal.

Practical Exercises for Chapter 15

Exercise 1 – The Letting Go Letter

Write a letter to someone or something you need to release. Pour out your feelings. Then destroy it in a safe way as a symbol of release.

Exercise 2 – Box Exercise

Keep a "worry box." Before bed, write your worries on slips of paper, place them in the box, and close it. Tell yourself: *"I'll deal with this tomorrow."*

Exercise 3 – Breath Release

Sit quietly. Inhale deeply. On each exhale, silently say: *"I release…"* and insert the name of what you're letting go (anger, regret, control).

Exercise 4 – Replace the Void

After releasing, immediately write down one positive activity you will do to fill the space. (Example: after letting go of regret, begin a gratitude journal.)

Key Lessons from This Chapter

* Holding on keeps you chained to the past—letting go sets you free.

* Forgiveness is not approval—it's liberation.

* Rituals make release tangible and lasting.

* Freedom is not just empty hands—it's choosing what new gifts to hold.

In the next chapter, we'll explore *The Power of Hope: Lighting the Path Forward*—because once you've let go of the past, you must lift your eyes toward a brighter future.

Chapter 16 – The Power of Hope: Lighting the Path Forward

"Hope is being able to see that there is light despite all of the darkness." – Desmond Tutu

Why Hope Is the Oxygen of the Soul

Fear steals your confidence.

Depression steals your joy.

But what they both fear most is **hope**.

Because hope is the oxygen of the soul. Without it, you suffocate in despair. With it, you can survive storms, endure suffering, and keep walking toward the light.

Hope does not mean denying pain. Hope means believing pain is not the end of the story.

Mini Story: The Girl With the Candle

In a war-torn village, a little girl was seen carrying a candle through the rubble at night. A soldier asked, *"Why bother with a candle when everything is destroyed?"*

She replied, *"Because even one candle can push back the dark."*

That is hope—not pretending the darkness doesn't exist, but refusing to let it win.

The Difference Between False Hope and Grounded Hope

Not all hope is equal.

* **False hope** says: "Nothing bad will ever happen again." (This sets you up for disappointment.)

* **Grounded hope** says: "Even when bad things happen, I will not give up. I will find a way forward."

Grounded hope is built on resilience, perspective, and faith that tomorrow can be better than today.

***"Once you choose hope, anything is possible."* – Christopher Reeve**

Step 1 – Imagine a Brighter Future

Fear and depression paint the future in dark colors. To fight back, you must **repaint your future in brighter shades.**

Visualization helps. Close your eyes and ask:

* What would my life look like if fear no longer ruled me?

* How would I feel waking up with peace instead of dread?

* Who would I become if depression no longer defined me?

Your brain doesn't know the difference between imagined and real experiences—visualizing hope plants seeds of possibility.

Mini Story: The Cancer Survivor

Ramesh was given six months to live. Doctors told him there was little chance. But he refused to stop hoping. Every morning he visualized himself playing cricket with his grandchildren.

He lived not six months—but six years. And in those years, he laughed, worked, and loved. He later said: *"Hope didn't cure my illness. But it gave me more life than fear ever could."*

Step 2 – Use Gratitude as Fuel for Hope

Gratitude reminds you of what is still good, even in difficulty.

Every time you say, *"I am grateful for this,"* you prove to your mind that not everything is lost.

Gratitude turns despair into perspective. And perspective feeds hope.

Step 3 – Surround Yourself With Hopeful People

Hope is contagious. So is hopelessness.

If you spend time with people who only complain, criticize, and predict doom—you'll sink.

Seek those who lift you, encourage you, and believe in possibility. Borrow their hope when yours runs low.

***"Hope is the companion of power, and mother of success."* – Samuel Smiles**

Step 4 – Anchor Your Hope in Symbols

Symbols are powerful reminders. Create your personal **“hope anchor.”**

* A photograph of someone you love.

* A quote on your wall.

* A song that makes you believe.

* A small object you carry in your pocket.

Whenever despair rises, touch your anchor. Let it remind you: *“I have reasons to keep going.”*

Mini Story: The Soldier’s Letter

During a long deployment, a young soldier battled depression and homesickness. What kept him alive was a single letter from his daughter. He carried it in his pocket, folded and worn.

Whenever despair hit, he touched that letter. *"It was my anchor,"* he said later. *"That letter kept me alive."*

Step 5 – Practice Daily Acts of Hope

Hope isn't just a feeling—it's a practice. You grow it by action.

* Get out of bed when you don't feel like it.

* Smile at someone.

* Start a new project.

* Take one small step toward a goal.

Each act whispers: *"The future still matters."*

Practical Exercises for Chapter 16

Exercise 1 – Future Letter

Write a letter from your future self (five years ahead) to your present self. Describe how you overcame challenges and built a brighter life.

Exercise 2 – Gratitude for Hope

Every morning, list three things you're grateful for. End each one with the phrase: *"...and this gives me hope."*

Exercise 3 – Hope Anchor

Choose a physical object, quote, or photo to symbolize hope. Keep it somewhere visible or carry it with you daily.

Exercise 4 – One Step Forward

Every day, take one small action that proves you believe in tomorrow. Track your steps for 21 days.

Key Lessons from This Chapter

* Hope is not denial—it's defiance against despair.

* False hope disappoints, but grounded hope empowers.

* Visualization, gratitude, hopeful people, and symbols all build lasting hope.

* Daily actions keep the flame alive even when darkness surrounds you.

In the next chapter, we'll explore *Living With Purpose: Turning Pain Into Power*—because hope is the spark, but purpose is the fire that sustains you for life.

Chapter 17

Living With Purpose: Turning Pain Into Power

"He who has a why to live can bear almost any how." – Friedrich Nietzsche

The Power of a Why

Fear paralyzes. Depression drains. But **purpose ignites.**

When you have a reason to wake up in the morning, life shifts. Even in pain, you find strength. Even in storms, you find direction.

Purpose doesn't erase suffering, but it gives suffering meaning. And meaning is often the bridge between despair and hope.

Mini Story: The Prisoner Who Found His Why

During World War II, Viktor Frankl was imprisoned in a concentration camp. Surrounded by death, hunger, and cruelty, many gave up on life. But Frankl survived. Why?

He wrote later: *"Those who have a 'why' to live can bear almost any 'how.'"*

His why was imagining himself giving lectures after the war, teaching others about the psychology of survival.

That purpose gave him strength in the darkest place on earth. His book, *Man's Search for Meaning,* has since inspired millions.

Step 1 – Understand What Purpose Really Is

Purpose is not just a big career goal or charity project. Purpose is meaning.

It can be:

* Raising your children with love.

* Creating beauty through art.

* Helping one person each day.

* Turning your pain into wisdom for others.

Purpose is not always loud. Sometimes it’s quiet, steady, and deeply personal.

"Your purpose in life is to find your purpose and give your whole heart and soul to it." – Buddha

Step 2 – Look Into Your Pain for Clues

Often, your deepest purpose is hidden inside your deepest wound.

* Survivors of depression become powerful encouragers.

* Those who lost loved ones often fight to save others from the same fate.

* People who suffered injustice become voices for justice.

Ask yourself: *“What pain in my past could I transform into service?”*

Mini Story: The Widow Who Chose Purpose

After losing her husband suddenly, Lakshmi fell into deep despair. For months she could barely function. But slowly, she asked: *"How can I use this pain?"*

She began a foundation in his memory, supporting widows who felt abandoned. Her grief didn't vanish, but it transformed. She said: *"My pain became my purpose. Helping others healed me, too."*

Step 3 – Discover Your Strengths and Passions

Purpose often lives where your strengths meet your passions.

* Strengths: What am I naturally good at?

* Passions: What lights me up inside?

* Needs: What does the world around me need?

When you connect these three, you begin to see your "why."

Step 4 – Start Small

You don't need to change the entire world to live with purpose. Start small.

* Call a friend who's struggling.

* Volunteer once a month.

* Create something that uplifts others.

* Share your story.

Purpose grows as you practice it.

"The meaning of life is to find your gift. The purpose of life is to give it away." – Pablo Picasso

Step 5 – Align Daily Life With Purpose

Living with purpose is not just about one big mission. It's about how you live every day.

* Do your words reflect kindness?

* Do your actions reflect love?

* Does your work reflect your values?

When even small actions align with your why, life feels meaningful.

Mini Story: The Teacher Who Taught Beyond Books

Suresh was a schoolteacher. At first, he thought his job was just about math and science. But when he realized his greater purpose was *"to inspire confidence in children,"* everything changed.

He began to encourage shy students, celebrate effort, and remind kids they were valuable. Years later, his students remembered not the lessons—but the way he made them believe in themselves.

That was his purpose.

Step 6 – Write Your Legacy

Ask yourself: *"How do I want to be remembered?"*

This isn't morbid—it's clarifying. Your legacy is not built at the end of life; it's built in everyday choices.

When you know the story you want your life to tell, you begin to live it with intention.

Practical Exercises for Chapter 17

Exercise 1 – Purpose Map

Draw three circles: Strengths, Passions, Needs. Write down items in each. Where they overlap—that's your purpose zone.

Exercise 2 – Pain to Purpose Journal

Write about one painful experience. Then ask: *"How could this pain help someone else?"* Brainstorm ways to turn it into service.

Exercise 3 – Legacy Letter

Write a letter as if you're at the end of your life, describing how you want to be remembered. Then ask: *"What's one action I can take today to live toward this legacy?"*

Exercise 4 – Daily Alignment

At night, reflect: *"Did my actions today align with my purpose?"* If not, how can tomorrow be closer?

Key Lessons from This Chapter

* Purpose gives meaning to suffering and strength to endure challenges.

* Your wounds often hold clues to your greatest calling.

* Purpose can be quiet, personal, and simple—it doesn't have to be world-shaking.

* Living on purpose is not one act—it's a way of living daily with alignment and intention.

In the next chapter, we'll conclude this journey with *The Ripple Effect: How Your Healing Helps the World*—because your purpose doesn't just transform you, it transforms everyone around you.

Chapter 18 – The Ripple Effect: How Your Healing Helps the World

"When you heal yourself, you heal the world."– Unknown

The Truth We Forget

When you battle fear and depression, it's easy to believe your life doesn't matter. That your healing is only for you. That your struggles are invisible, isolated, and meaningless.

But here is the truth: **Every step you take toward healing creates ripples far beyond your own life.**

When you rise, others rise.

When you shine, others see the way.

When you heal, you give others permission to heal too.

Your journey is not just personal—it is generational, communal, and world-changing.

Mini Story: The Mother Who Broke the Chain

Radhika grew up in a family of silence and suppressed pain. Her mother battled depression but never sought help. Radhika herself struggled with anxiety as an adult.

But one day, she made a decision: *"The cycle ends with me."* She began therapy, practiced mindfulness, and slowly found peace.

Her children noticed. They saw a mother who could talk about feelings, who modeled self-care, who loved herself enough to set boundaries.

Years later, her daughter said: *"Because of you, I know how to face my own struggles."*

Radhika didn't just heal herself. She changed her entire family's future.

The Ripple of Presence

When you are calmer, your presence changes the atmosphere around you.

* A smile given at the right moment can save a life.

* A kind word spoken can lift a heavy heart.

* Your peaceful energy can influence a whole room.

Healing doesn't always look dramatic. Sometimes it's as simple as walking into a space and bringing light with you.

"If you think you are too small to make a difference, try sleeping in a room with a mosquito." – African Proverb

Step 1 – Realize Your Influence

You influence people every day—whether you notice or not.

* The way you speak to a stranger.

* The way you treat yourself in front of your children.

* The way you listen to a friend.

Even in small moments, your healing ripples outward.

Step 2 – From Wounded to Warrior

Your scars are not shameful—they are sacred.

When you share your story of overcoming fear or depression, you may give someone else the courage to fight another day.

Never underestimate the power of saying: *"I've been there too, and I made it."*

Mini Story: The Young Man at the Bridge

A man once stood on a bridge, ready to end his life. But a stranger walked past, smiled at him, and said: *"Are you okay?"*

That small act broke the darkness for him. He later said: *"That smile saved my life. It reminded me I wasn't invisible."*

One moment. One ripple. One life saved.

Step 3 – Healing Is Contagious

Science shows that emotions are contagious. If you are anxious, those around you feel it. If you are peaceful, others relax too.

When you practice healing, you don't just change yourself—you shift the emotional atmosphere of your family, your workplace, and your community.

Step 4 – Generational Ripples

When you learn to release fear, practice self-compassion, and live with purpose, you pass that wisdom on.

* Your children learn resilience.

* Your friends feel inspired.

* Your community sees possibility.

Generational trauma is real—but so is **generational healing.**

***"The world changes when we change."* – Unknown**

Step 5 – Service as the Final Ripple

The ultimate ripple of healing is service.

When you turn your growth into action for others, your life becomes a beacon.

* Mentoring someone younger.

* Volunteering your time.

* Creating art that uplifts.

* Simply living kindly, daily.

Your life becomes not just about survival, but contribution.

Mini Story: The Teacher Who Started With One Child

A teacher named Manoj once noticed a shy, struggling student. He decided to give her extra attention, encouragement, and kindness. That girl later became a successful doctor—and told Manoj, *"You changed my life."*

Manoj smiled and said: *"I just helped one student."*

But what he didn't realize was that his ripple now touches every patient she heals.

Practical Exercises for Chapter 18

Exercise 1 – Ripple Journal

Each night, write down one way your actions may have positively impacted someone else

Exercise 2 – Share Your Story

Tell someone you trust about one struggle you've overcome. Notice how sharing connects you and gives them hope.

Exercise 3 – Generational Healing Letter

Write a letter to your future children or loved ones, describing the lessons you are learning in healing. This becomes a gift to the next generation.

Exercise 4 – Act of Service

Once a week, do one intentional act of service (helping a neighbor, listening deeply, encouraging a friend). Track the ripple it creates.

Key Lessons from This Chapter

* Your healing is not just for you—it is for everyone connected to you.

* Even small acts of peace and kindness create life-changing ripples.

* Your scars can inspire others when you share them with courage.

* Healing spreads through families, communities, and generations.

A Final Word: You Are the Ripple

The world does not change only through big speeches, famous leaders, or grand revolutions.

The world changes through ordinary people who choose to heal, to live with hope, to embody love.

That person is you.

Every step you take—letting go, finding hope, living with purpose—creates ripples that touch lives you may never even see.

So never doubt it: **Your healing is world-changing.**

And when fear whispers *"You don't matter,"* let your life answer loudly: *"Watch my ripples."*

Conclusion – A New Beginning

"And suddenly you know: it's time to start something new and trust the magic of beginnings." – Meister Eckhart

This Is Not the End

You have walked through the pages of this book with courage. You have faced fear, wrestled with depression, and chosen the path of healing. You have learned how to let go, how to build hope, how to live with purpose, and how your healing creates ripples in the world.

But let me remind you: **this is not the end of your journey. This is the beginning.**

Books end. Pages close. But life continues—and now, you are equipped with tools, stories, and practices to transform the rest of your journey.

The Three Truths to Carry Forward

If you remember nothing else from this book, let it be these truths:

1. **You Are Not Broken.**

Fear and depression may have told you lies about your worth. But you are not broken—you are becoming. Every scar is proof of survival, every struggle is part of your growth.

2. **You Have Power to Choose.**

You cannot always choose your circumstances, but you can always choose your response. In every moment, you hold the power to breathe, to hope, to act, and to rise.

3. **Your Healing Matters Beyond You.**

You are not small. Your journey is not meaningless. The healing you create in yourself will echo through families, friendships, communities, and generations.

"The wound is the place where the Light enters you." – Rumi

The New You

Think back to when you first picked up this book. Maybe you felt stuck. Maybe fear ruled your thoughts. Maybe depression whispered lies in the dark.

Now, imagine yourself today:

* You have tools to calm your mind.

* You have learned to let go of burdens.

* You have rediscovered hope.

* You have found a sense of purpose.

This is the new you—not perfect, not without challenges, but stronger, wiser, and freer.

Mini Story: The Bamboo Tree

In China, there is a species of bamboo that takes five years to break the ground. For years, farmers water and nurture it, seeing nothing. Then, in the fifth year, it suddenly shoots up more than eighty feet in just weeks.

Life is like that bamboo. Your healing may feel slow, invisible, frustrating. But beneath the surface, roots are growing. And one day, your breakthrough will rise higher than you imagined.

So keep watering. Keep nurturing. Keep believing.

A Call to Action: Live What You've Learned

Knowledge without action is like a seed never planted.

Now it's time to put into practice what you've learned.

Here are five daily commitments you can carry forward:

1. **Breathe with Awareness.** Even one mindful breath pulls you into the present.

2. **Let Go of One Burden Each Day.** Release anger, regret, or fear—little by little.

3. **Practice Gratitude.** Write three things each day you are thankful for.

4. **Choose Hopeful Actions.** Take one step daily that proves you believe in tomorrow.

5. **Serve with Purpose.** Do one act of kindness or service each week.

Small daily actions create lifelong transformation.

Your Legacy Starts Now

Imagine yourself ten years from now, looking back on this moment. Will you remember it as the day you read another book? Or as the day you decided to live differently?

Legacy is not built someday—it's built today. It's built in how you love, how you heal, and how you live your purpose.

"What you do makes a difference, and you have to decide what kind of difference you want to make." – Jane Goodall

The Final Ripple

You may never know the full impact of your healing. You may never meet the people whose lives you change with your smile, your kindness, your courage.

But make no mistake: **you are creating ripples.**

* A child will feel safer because you learned peace.

* A friend will feel stronger because you shared hope.

* A stranger may live another day because you smiled.

And generations from now, someone may thrive because you chose to heal today.

A Blessing for Your Journey

As you close this book, I want to leave you with these words:

May you let go of fear and walk in freedom.

May you rise from depression and dance with hope.

May your scars become stories of courage.

May your life shine so brightly that others find their way in your light.

And may you never forget—

**You are stronger than your fear.

You are greater than your depression.

You are a ripple that can change the world.**

This is your new beginning. Live it fully

Dear Friend,

If you are reading this final page, I want you to pause for a moment and feel proud of yourself. You stayed with this journey, you opened your heart to new truths, and you chose healing when fear and depression tried to hold you back. That is no small thing. That is courage.

When I began writing this book, my deepest wish was simple: that one person, somewhere, might pick up these words and feel less alone. If this book has helped you in any way—if it gave you hope, peace, or even one tool you could use in your life—then every hour spent writing was worth it.

But remember: this is not goodbye. Healing is not a one-time event; it is a lifelong practice. And you do not have to walk it alone.

Please keep reminding yourself of these truths:

* You are not broken—you are becoming.

* You are stronger than your fear.

* You are more than your depression.

* And you are deeply worthy of love, joy, and freedom.

If you ever doubt that, return to these pages. Let them remind you of the strength you already carry inside.

Finally, I invite you to stay connected with me. I'll continue writing, sharing, and walking this path alongside you. Whether it's through my next book, letters, or future teachings—I would be honored to be part of your journey.

Until then, live with courage, with hope, and with purpose.

And never forget—**you are the ripple that can change the world.**

With love and gratitude,

Dr. Abhijit Sharma

NEW BOOK RECOMMENDATION...

TRAIN YOUR
BRAIN
TO BE
HAPPY
21 days life changing exercises on How to be Happy
INTERNATIONAL
BEST
SELLER
DR. ABHIJIT SHARMA

Freedom from
Fear & Depression
WORKBOOK
Daily Worksheets and Tools to Break
Free from Fear, Negative Thinking,
and Emotional Struggles
DR. ABHIJIT SHARMA

BEST SELLER
Anxiety
Therapy
for men
Heal Yourself in 21 Days
DR. ABHIJIT SHARMA

www.ingramcontent.com/pod-product-compliance
Lightning Source LLC
Chambersburg PA
CBHW050016170726
48282CB00025B/430
* 9 7 8 9 3 3 4 3 8 6 7 5 2 *